# Sally's Scary Halloween

by

## wjHughes

wjHughes is in fact Dr. William Hughes,
family physician and grandfather,
living in New Mexico with his wife Vicky.

ISBN-13: 978-1495970597

# Sally's Scary Halloween

Dedicated to Delaney
and all my grandchildren
who keep my imagination bubbling
and my life a joy.

Sally Palmer was in the second grade. She usually woke up on school mornings in a very good mood. She especially liked crisp, cool autumn mornings. She could see the changing colors and smell the scents of the fall season.

Sally went to Lee Samuel Hollow Grade School. She walked there every morning with her friends, Lisha and Henry.

Their teacher was Ms. Eddings, whom they thought was very nice, as well as very smart. They thought she was fun too. Like last year, she brought a sled dog to class on the first day it snowed.

Or how she brought a hutch of rabbits to class just before Easter.

This fall, Sally noticed all the Halloween decorations in the classroom. She still had to decide on a costume for the night of trick or treat.

The next day at school, Sally thought something was different. She wasn't sure what, but she talked to Lisha about Halloween at recess and on the way home from school.

When the children went to class the following day, Ms. Eddings did not look well. Her face was greenish yellow, and Sally thought her hair was darker. And was her nose longer and pointier? Sally was confused. So was Henry.

Sally, Henry, and Lisha hurried to school the next day. Ms. Eddings was writing on the board. She was wearing a strange hat and her dress was gray. Her hair was black and stringy. Her back looked rounded.

When Ms. Eddings turned around, her skin looked green. Her nose was pointy with a bump on the end. There was a bump on her chin, and she had crooked, somewhat sharp, teeth. She looked *SCARY!*

"How are you, my dearies?" she asked. Then she laughed – cackled, really – and positively loomed over the front row desks.

All the children ran for the door. Down the school hallway they went, to the principal's office.

The principal stopped the children and asked what they were doing. "It's Ms. Eddings," said Sally. "She's different! We are afraid to go back."

"Let's go see what is going on," replied the principal.
"I'm sure you are mistaken."

Back in the classroom, Ms. Eddings was sitting at her desk, a broom in one hand, a tissue in the other. "Welcome back, dearies," she said.

"See," said Sally to the principal. "She's ... different!"

"Whatever are you talking about?" Ms. Eddings said. She was rubbing her face with the tissue. Her face was changing! There was pink showing through the yellow- green skin.

She stood up and took off her hat. She grabbed her straggly hair, and it came off! Sally and all the children looked on with wide eyes and open mouths.

Ms. Eddings tugged at her nose and it ended up in her hand. She reached to her back and pulled out a pillow from under her gown.

Sally realized what had happened.

"Ms. Eddings is back!" Lisha exclaimed.

"She was never gone!"

"That was the best trick I ever saw on Halloween," said Henry.

"I hope our treats are just as good!" replied Sally.

"Happy Halloween!" said Ms. Eddings as she brought out a bag of goodies for the whole class.